Reality Changes With the Willy Nilly Wind

poems by

Susan Huebner

Finishing Line Press
Georgetown, Kentucky

Reality Changes With the Willy Nilly Wind

Copyright © 2018 by Susan Huebner
ISBN 978-1-63534-518-6 First Edition
All rights reserved under International and Pan-American Copyright Conventions. No part of this book may be reproduced in any manner whatsoever without written permission from the publisher, except in the case of brief quotations embodied in critical articles and reviews.

ACKNOWLEDGMENTS

Balloon Bouquet at Library Square ~ *BROAD!* Online Literary Journal, Summer 2014
Winter's Schedule ~ *It's About Time* anthology, Main Street Rag, Fall 2016
Autumn Shadows ~ *Wisconsin Poets' Calendar* 2015
Tending To ~ *The Transition Issue*, Here Comes Everyone 2015
Spirit Bridge ~ *Lost: Reflections Anthology*, Medusa's Laugh Press 2016
Predictable Happenstance ~ *Wisconsin Poets' Calendar* 2018

Publisher: Leah Maines
Editor: Christen Kincaid
Cover Art and Design: Kurt John Huebner
Author Photo: Susan Martell Huebner

Printed in the USA on acid-free paper.
Order online: www.finishinglinepress.com
               also available on amazon.com

                     Author inquiries and mail orders:
                           Finishing Line Press
                             P. O. Box 1626
                       Georgetown, Kentucky 40324
                                U. S. A.

Table of Contents

Balloon Bouquet at Library Square 1

Winter's Schedule 3

When the Phone Rings Late at Night 4

Autumn Shadows 5

February Thaw 6

Reality Changes with the Willy-Nilly Wind but the Story

    Remains True 7

Big Ears, Nosey Rosy, Banjo Eyes 8

Tending To 10

Powder Puff Consequences 11

Prey 13

Beyond the Grave 14

Corralling the Bells 15

On the Line 17

Fall Memories 19

Dining in the Memory Unit 20

Spirit Bridge 21

When Father Tom Comes to Anoint the Sick 22

Predictable Happenstance 24

*With gratitude to Mary Rose
and Theresa
for the journey we took
together*

Balloon Bouquet at Library Square

I.
At the senior living facility where my mother now lives
in the entrance lobby, wide as a ballroom and cheerfully quiet as a church
3 balloons strain against their weighted ribbons, longing for release.
Each is a shiny silver number: 1 0 0.
Someone has hit the century mark.

The doors woosh open and close with comings and goings.
Every soft, breezy swoosh sends the puffed-proud mylar puppets dancing
floating in the weak winter sun streaming through the windows.

II.
These days my mother floats, too
riding the wind horse of memory.
Sometimes she controls the reins,
cherishes the radiance of her good fortune.
Those are worry-free days.
But sometimes the destinations that call
are not of her choosing.
Those days are blue blankets
she pulls up to her chin.

III.
I give my mother a set of towels, bright flowers embroidered on soft
Egyptian cotton.
She treasures these, keeps them folded in tissue paper in her closet.
They're too special, she says, to be used for everyday.
In her bathroom hang threadbare towels I remember from my childhood.
On her bed, a white plastic basket filled with fresh laundry waiting
to be placed in lilac-sachet drawers.

Worn gossamer-thin, a pair of flannel pajamas sits atop a nightgown,
one my father loved, lacy trim at the hem now attached by safety pins.
No, she says, she doesn't really need new pajamas. She has plenty.

IV.
I am not always prepared
to enter the fragile shrine of her last home.
Sometimes when I leave her
I sit in the parking lot and weep.
I think about the balloons,
the great three-digit miracle
that someone, not my mother, celebrates.
I try to believe that today
is celebration enough.

Winter's Schedule

Late January in Wisconsin
and the television is not working.
My mother watches the snow,
the only show available.

A banshee wind throws slaps of slush
on her balcony and covers summer's geranium baskets.
The drifts reach the windowsills of the first floor units.

Without Lawrence Welk, how can she dream-dance with Dad?
Without the deep vibrato of Raymond Burr's voice, how to feel safe?
Without the pseudo-cheer of the late afternoon news,
how to find her place on the map of the world?

She knows the riskiest place to live
is in the too-quiet apartment of a new year.
She understands she is but a guest in her body.
She senses, more than knows, that her memories are stardust
gossiping within the closed covers of family albums.

Tomorrow the sun will shine through the slatted blinds,
strips of fire across the living room carpet.
She'll try the TV one more time,
pick up the remote, aim for another day.

When the Phone Rings Late at Night

My sister keeps saying
We're next, ya know
and I text her SHUT UP
and mean it
but feel the message
clicking clear
fast
vibrating
in the palm of my hand

Autumn Shadows

we drive the country road
trees whisper into the cobalt sky
leaves drift like wishes onto the windshield

in the passenger seat
my mother, lovely as a cloud
silver-grey hair, pastel pink bow soft at her throat

I wonder if she's thinking of her husband
my father who died
on a day stamped in brilliance
just like this

she watches the golds and reds roll across the hills
says, *I hope when I go, I don't die in winter*
I ask her why
she says *I don't know*
and raises a hand to the grandness
It's just so pretty this time of year

February Thaw

Phone calls won't soothe her. Mother wants to see me so I drive to pick her up.

Today she answers the door attired for our adventure: clip-on earrings, Cleopatra-red lipstick, salt and pepper cowlick tamed and acting Sunday-best, for the moment. She's taken great care.

Her walker is ready to roll out, its pink floral purse packed with the necessities: tissues, wallet, keys, a plastic sandwich bag filled with lemon drops. It sits parked, blocking my way into the apartment. She's eager to jump the fence of her compressed life, doesn't want to linger.

Let's go, she says.

We negotiate the long hall toward the lobby, along the way admire door décor. At one, a seasonally dressed lady goose, bonnet tied primly under her chin. At some, shiny foil shamrocks anticipate tomorrow. At others, Valentine hearts hold on to yesterday. Some are blank faces. We don't comment on these.

Finally at the entry, the doors whoosh open. We step into fresh air and she pauses at the curb. Her hands firmly on the metal frame, she leans forward, inhales, closes her eyes, smiles.

I smell spring, she says.

I know the warm Trade Winds of her first kiss and my father's long-absent embrace are calling to her. But for today's needs, I help her into my car, crack a window. We go to lunch.

reality changes with the willy nilly wind but the story remains true

I.
your sister in California joins us for fish fry in Wisconsin
but only you see her seated at our table
I learn this later   when I overhear you telling a friend
But right now   I am oblivious   I pass you the rye bread
pads of butter   try to keep a cheery dialogue   how is your trout
do you like the potato salad   is your back feeling better   you startle
suddenly discover me   a strange planet orbiting in your world
you cover your mouth with a napkin   focus on my face
then relax   settle deeper into your chair   you've come back
from wherever you've travelled

II.
though I cover more cleverly   I know I can exit just as swiftly
I am twelve years old   peeking through a screen window   I
discover you   bathing before a porcelain basin   you stand on
the linoleum floor   it beams beneath a swaying lightbulb   I
hear the chain clinking in the breeze   see you naked   white
skin   Sicilian dark hair   brown nipples   so awesome and
strange a sight yet I feel   something familiar stir inside me
your veined hand pats my arm   you gesture for the salt shaker
I reach for it   I am back

III.
and here we are
I am not twelve   you are not young
I cannot help but see your crooked spine
you cannot help but take my hand
we are not always in the same time
when at the same place
but there are those moments
the boundaries still permeable
when we join each other
drifting in the same dream

Big Ears, Nosey Rosy, Banjo Eyes
the words you used for my curiosity.

Big Ears, earned for the times you caught me listening to your conversations with Dad when you sat at the kitchen table after supper. I knew the quieter the voices, the juicier the talk: about Dad's too Catholic, too perfect sisters; about his tobacco-spitting father, our grandpa who visited always needing a coffee can placed at his feet for his brown spittle. Even though I sometimes sat two rooms away pretending to read, face hidden behind my ubiquitous library book, somehow you knew and would say *Big Ears is listening* and then the scrape of chairs as you rose from the table, the sound of water running to rinse coffee cups ending the conversation.

Nosey Rosy earned for those times I hung around near the wall phone in the kitchen while your voice grew loud with exasperation, sometimes with anger telling family tales we children were not to repeat. I understand, now, your loneliness and need to share, but I didn't, then; you seemed disloyal. *I'll call you when Nosey Rosy is in school* ended those conversations.

Banjo Eyes, for those times when I was not tired, did not want to be put to bed on a perfect summer afternoon, told to take a nap, be a good example for the little ones. *Close those big banjo eyes so your sisters will do the same. You're the oldest. I count on you.* It was torture then, told to do nothing when the wide world hummed with words and vibrated with possibility. But I understand, now. You needed a small space of quiet away from our demanding eyes where you could rest, splash cool water on your face, try to remember the carefree girl, before you became the harried mother.

Today I use Banjo Eyes to watch you age, watch for the small hesitations in body or voice that might mean a doctor's visit or maybe an extra pillow; Nosey Rosy to inspect your refrigerator for expiration dates on milk cartons, check your calendar to remind you of penny bingo in the dining room, a grandchild's upcoming birthday you would feel terrible to miss. Big Ears to hear the words you say, the words you use now when talking to me.

My darling girl, I count on you. My eldest daughter, what would I do without you?

Tending To

A lot goes into this tending idea
        To take care of
        To nurture
        To protect
        To encourage
People and plants need a lot of this verb
Sometimes, this means dealing with shit:
        I spade cow manure to enrich the soil
        Hose bird poop polka-dots off my car
        Call carpet cleaners for human crap
        when digestive tracts malfunction
        Trash nightgowns, undies, sometimes sheets
Sometimes, this means stripping:
        I pull sucker leaves from stems
        Wrap bark on fruit trees to protect them
        I worry about Mother's increasing ability
        to forget she is not dressed as
when she opens her apartment door
wearing but a camisole and I follow
her wrinkled little butt cheeks so sweet
so vulnerable and I am glad once again
it is me and not the maintenance man
who's knocked upon her door.

Powder Puff Consequences

Mom cannot leave her apartment without fixing her face. Traversing the long hallway for penny bingo or for lunch and dinner, or to partake in exercise classes or to check her mail—all require a certain look. The look is set in powder, Cover Girl compact #130.

She stands before her mirror, swipes the puff across her face and up and down. Over and over, swipes puff over powder, swipes puff over face, forehead, chin, nose, cheekbones, includes eyelids. My eyes feel scratchy watching her. *We're going to be late for lunch* I say.

I'm almost ready she answers. *I just need my lipstick.* She's a good three minutes from ready. I know how long it takes her to apply the ruby red, #42. When she's finally done, I check her teeth. No lipstick. Good. And she's remembered to put in her partial. Good. *Let's boogie, Mom. They've started serving lunch.* I am an hour beyond hungry.

It's not a problem she says. *They'll take our menu whenever we get there.* But there is a problem. Her usual table is full up. No room for us. Her regular meal companions smile at us and wave. The unusual one, a man, acknowledges us with a nod. Mom parks her walker behind him, looking put out. I gesture to an empty table next to us, try to pre-empt what I know is coming. She allows me to guide her into a chair, take her walker, seat her. She stares at the man. *He's in my seat* she says, loudly enough for those with good ears to hear. Thankfully, those ears do not seem to apply to the man in *her* seat. The server approaches, takes our orders. *We both want the chicken entrée* I say. *We do?* Mom asks. *The other choice is chili macaroni casserole* I tell her.

I want the chicken she says, and, with a queenly gesture, hands the menu to the server, asks her *Who is that man? He is in my seat.* The server reiterates what I have already said, that he is a resident, that there are no assigned seats. I try to redirect. *That fruit cup looks good, Mom.* She picks at it. When the rest of the food arrives, I pick at the scoop of dehydrated mashed potatoes and try to disassemble the lukewarm hunk of chicken thigh with attached wing. It's not worth the effort, but I am hungry. *Why don't they flavor anything in this place* I complain. *I wonder why that man is in my seat* she answers.

Lunch ends and the man pushes himself away from the table. He reaches for his cane and rises to limp out of the dining room. Mom watches, boring holes into his back. *That poor man* I say. *He looks like it is hard for him to navigate.* Mom turns and trains her eyes on me. I know what she's thinking.

Later, I am on an elliptical at the YMCA when my husband dismounts his treadmill and walks over to me on his way to the weight room. *I almost didn't see you* he says. *You're not on your usual machine.* I tell him it was occupied when I arrived. He jokes *You should have kicked the person off, told them it is your machine.*

It's okay I say. *It's really, really okay.*

Prey

Mother's table mates have begun to notice
when she starts to drift away
One squawks *A penny for your thoughts*
and I am tempted to scold him
say she cannot sell her thoughts so cheaply
I cannot tell if he means to pull her back to shore
toward safe moorings of conversation or
if he means to crow
Look at how crazy she's getting
How smart I am to point it out

I would offer a bucket of gold
at the end of a rainbow for her thoughts
that sometimes rise from clear skies
the ones ringing with brightness
of wind chimes in April

These are the rare thoughts

More remain which are cloudy
behind eyes milky with cataracts
jumping synapses from right now to long ago
like the scatter of squirrels at the feeder
when hawk shadow passes over

Beyond the Grave

My uncle calls to tell me he's learned
that he's recently deceased.
Yes, I say, *despite what we assure Mother*
she believes you've permanently left the building.

We laugh. What else is there to do?

Mother bemoans she never hears from Father's side anymore
forgets two sisters-in-law are gone, three brothers-in-law too
forgets the living relatives are decades old as she
one aunt with dementia, another barely still able to drive.

Some memories she lives with as present tense.
Asks where her car is now, wants to renew her license.
Calls from her apartment to say *Who's coming to pick me up?*
I have to check out of this hotel by nine.

I tell my uncle he's off the hook for visiting.
She can't remember when you've come over
that you just took her to lunch, attended her birthday
or that you've called, evidently, from beyond the grave.

We laugh.

What else is there to do?

Corralling the Bells

There are cheery red felt bows over each entry doorway and several decorate the check-in window. The sign-in pen is taped to a plastic poinsettia rather than the usual plastic spoon. On this day the lobby is empty of wheelchairs and canes and those who propel them; everyone is moving toward the area set for the performance. There is shuffling and chair sliding as the residents jostle in to wait. We, the more easily mobile, walk toward the crowd, wave at the people we recognize to let them know we are here. I smile and widely gesture hello to one particular face I see searching for me. It is my mother.

When the director walks into the dining room, it is as royalty: back straight, head held high, eyes forward, looking neither right nor left. She takes her place before the seated elderly women. Her back is to us, the audience. The room settles into a silence broken only by a man loudly blowing his nose. It sounds like a moose call, and some people snicker.

The director ignores it. She is all business, white hair pulled into a bun at her nape and wearing a red holiday scarf tied into a bow which rests on her crisp white blouse. It covers her chest, although, if she were asked, she would say bosom. We, the invited relatives and friends, sit scattered among round tables. Some of the people who live here could be our former neighbors; most are our parents or grandparents or elderly aunts and uncles. We've turned our padded chairs the best we can manage to face the chimers.

Now it's time. The director raises her arms, elbows bent, hands in the air. Her chimers hold bells at attention upon their shoulders, their eyes upon her, bright as birds, though it is a brightness of excitement rather than sharp focus. They look ready, for the most part, but there is a stirring at one end of the row. A chimer has put down her hand bell to adjust her scarf. We see the director's head turn toward the elderly wiggler. Her wiggling stops. She picks up her bell.

The director's head moves again, ever so slightly, to center and her eyes sweep over her assembled flock. She thrusts a finger toward one player and the notes begin to tinkle into the vast room. Each pointing jab produces one lovely vibration followed by another. The notes fall like snowflakes around us, at a pace just fast enough that we can pull them together into a melody. It is "The Carol of the Bells."

The chimers are into their performance, each one scooping her bell energetically into the air, then setting it to rest upon her shoulder, awaiting its next command performance. Some smile and some sway to the music. Then it happens. Two chimers play at once, one playing the note anticipated; the other playing a flat surprise. The director's finger doesn't stop or even slow down; she keeps pointing, deliberate, demanding, at each chimer, and the music goes on. But there has been a tiny avalanche, and more wrong notes follow, as if each stumbles into the wrong boot print in deep snow.

We sit and pretend as if nothing untoward is happening. The director pretends the same. We hold our collective breath and will them to recover. They mostly do, playing through to the end. When the music finishes, we clap our appreciation and the chimers struggle to standing to take their bows. They rise individually more than as a group as some reach for a cane or grab on to the chairs before them for a needed boost. The director turns and bows, too. Her face is stern, her bun still neatly intact at the nape of her neck.

We applaud until our palms sting. My mother's face glows.

On the Line

I.
clothespins in my mouth
wet whaps of cool cloth on my bare arms
the game I play with the wind when hanging
sheets outside on the clothesline

at night I lay my cheek on cotton
that holds the faint sweet echoes of buzzing bees
the scents of grass and tang of almost-fall marigolds
Mmmm mmmm outdoor sheets my husband hums
we hold hands and drift into our dreams

II.
crossing the line
lines in the sand
everything on the line
Step on a crack and you break your mother's back
we sang as children
our latest line crossed with a signature
that placed mother into Home Hospice

III.
I draw the line
when hearing the caregiver talk
about Mother and not to her
My mother's not a lamp I tell her
Dementia doesn't mean deaf
she apologizes but I see the hard
line in her eyes and know
she doesn't mean it

IV.
thinking about impermanence
lines drawn in the sand
so easily washed away
bottom lines that bottom out
like soggy brown grocery bags
which break and spill across
my driveway and I chase a cantaloupe
down the asphalt incline careful
to step over and not on the cracks

Fall Memories

colors burst like synapses firing
against the strident blue sky

mother notices
over and over how lovely
the trees outside her window

it's a new window in a new locale for her
as yet there is yet no accounting for
the number of steps before reaching the bathroom
the different faces at her table in the dining room
the startling alarm of the bracelet on her ankle
she says *I'm safe here*
because that's what we've told her

but

she wonders
where her keys have gone
wants to lock her apartment door

and

we wonder
whether she can adjust

we see the bruises of falls she does not recall
we're told how she wanders through her nights
the need to move always upon her
propelling her along carpeted hallways
seeking some familiar place

until the sun rises
and the colors call her home
to gentler times when falls meant
the stunning into prayer
and a resting place for her heart

Dining in the Memory Unit

Using wheelchairs or walkers, canes or their own strong limbs
they push themselves away from the tables, move in single file
down the hallway, a parade without music or audience
no cheerful salutations for later nor the balm of eye contact
they peel off the obedient line one by one and enter their rooms

Those who served now clean up, in practiced pirouettes
they gather plates and saucers, sweep crumbs into their soft
palms quietly as afternoon snowflakes, set dishes into
washing racks with not even a companionable clink of cup
to cup, silverware gently into shallow plastic bins denying
even the cutlery its happy clatter
nothing disturbs the settled fog

But, one day at lunch, silver-haired Tony raises his voice
at table, sings out an Italian *volare!*, his vibrato makes
the orange Jello shiver in its bowls, forks pause midway
to mouths, the room bursts into applause and cries of
more, more ring into the air, except for Frank who
frowns even deeper, grumbles *go sing near a window so
we can help you out* and continues eating his pot pie

Spirit Bridge

Daily, my sister and I search
travel across the mists of our
mother's memories seeking solid
ground on which to reach her
anchor her with us here

the expanse grows wider
her questions more repetitive
our conversations now
the same sad chanting
of call and response

she is drifting toward
the place we cannot follow
a time she resides in behind
her eyes with those she remembers
so clearly who beckon her

While daily, my sister and I
seek and hold steady
the best we know how
the bridge she treads softly
where we cannot follow

When Father Tom Comes to Anoint the Sick

the sacrament which used to be
known as Extreme Unction or
The Last Rites

he asks Mother if she perhaps
wants to confess her sins
this woman whose wants she

sometimes knows other times
can barely express but always
politely she answers *I suppose*

we leave them alone to confer
in private the man schooled
in abstraction and doctrine

he waits to hear from
our mother whose desires now
tend toward the concrete

half & half in her coffee
oatmeal cookies to dunk
a small dish of warm prunes

one of us to hold her hand
place an afghan on her feet
answer when she inquires

of people some alive some
passed on the living the dead
now present the same

we tell her of course yes
your mother will come soon
our father and brother as well

we wait outside her apartment
wonder what possible sins
the priest might absolve

for a woman who's walked ninety
years on this earth and surely
by now has paid for them all

Predictable Happenstance

rabbits eat the beet tops when your back is turned
weeds sprout defiant overnight in your raised bed plot
your mother grows fragile as a snowdrop that glistens
in early March then leaves to allow
the blossoming of spring

Susan **Martell Huebner** lives in Mukwonago, WI and writes looking out upon a tall white birch in her front yard. She has a tabby named Chin Chin to keep her company and who occasionally blocks both the view out her window as well as her computer screen.

Susan has been writing for most of her life and credits receiving acknowledgement for an essay she wrote as an eighth grader (and winning a prize of two dollars!) as the beginning of her lifelong passion with putting words on paper.

Her poetry has appeared in both print and online publications as well as in several anthologies. Cawing Crow Press published her literary novel *She Thought the Door Was Locked*, an excerpt of which can be read on her website. She is a member of the Wisconsin Fellowship of Poets as well as Wisconsin Writers Association, and writes in community with a talented and generous group of people at ALLWRITERS' WORKPLACE & WORKSHOP. Many of the pieces in this chapbook originated in Door County at Poetry Camp and were polished with help from the remarkable poets who meet there yearly to create and laugh.

She enjoys collaborating with her nature photographer husband, Kurt, who designed the cover for this chapbook. His photography, as well as examples of Susan's poetry, can be found on her website www.susanmhuebner.com.

www.ingramcontent.com/pod-product-compliance
Lightning Source LLC
LaVergne TN
LVHW041519070426
835507LV00012B/1696